ADULTISH

A TWENTY-SOMETHING-F*CK'S STORIES AND POEMS

CARLOS LERMA

CARLOS LERMA

Copyright © 2024 by Carlos Lerma

All rights reserved. No part of this publication may be reproduced, distributed, or transmitted in any form or by any means, including photocopying, recording, or other electronic or mechanical methods, without the prior written permission of the publisher, except in the case of brief quotations embodied in critical reviews and certain other noncommercial uses permitted by copyright law.

For permission requests, write to the publisher at the address below:

hello@carloselerma.com
www.carloselerma.com

ISBN: 979-8-8690-8911-3

Visit www.carloselerma.com for more information about the author and upcoming releases.

Author and Illustrator: Carlos Lerma
Interior Layout and Design: Carlos Lerma

Third Edition: June, 2024

ALSO BY CARLOS LERMA

POETRY

Underdog Days (2022)

SHORT STORIES

Identity Thief (2021)
Call Me Crazy (2021)
Luigi's Pizza (2021)

POETRY IN SPANISH

Sueños & Desastres (2021)
Anomalía (2020)
Buenas Historias de Malos Días (2019)

To the new twenty-something-fucks
trying to get through the day.
We'll be okay.

FOREWORD

Never in the last nineteen years would I see myself as being in my twenties. Growing up is one of those things you don't worry about as a child, but hope comes sooner rather than later. As children, we see the fun things in growing up. The things we can't do then.

As an adult, I can get whatever I want at the grocery store, but now I battle myself over the brand of eggs that's cheaper instead of what ice cream flavor I want. Now, I hate seeing my room messy even though I do this to myself and then clean it up. When I wake up late, I now feel like I wasted an entire morning when I could've been productive.

The bullies who once made fun of me for drawing and writing away in the back of the classroom, making silly videos and movies, or being an all-around artsy kid now look in envy at what I do.

Kids hate the loser, while adults hate the winner. I'm not saying I've won, but I don't see the people wanting me to fail on the field.

Gone are the Underdog Days, for the Adultish years are here.

It's been a long while since I spoke to you, dear friend, in book form. I last wrote a book when I was seventeen years old and living in Mexico. I wrote all of my books secluded from the world in my childhood bedroom. Since then, my life has gone through quite a few changes to say the least.

I've grown into an adultish man.

There are so many things I've felt I was too scared to talk about in previous books. Actual relationships, my sexuality, genuine arguments, ruptures, self-esteem issues, longing, being the villain, and living alone.

I could not touch on some because I never experienced them, others because I had not moved yet, others because I was too afraid, others because I was a virgin.

I've discovered what love actually is. I've found love in true friendships with people that I know will visit me when I'm put in a home.

Growing up has taught me a lot about not caring what people see me for. To some, I'm the best friend in the world. To some, I'm a generous person. To some, I'm just a funny guy they see occasionally. To some, I'm an annoying piece of shit that promotes their work a lot on social media. To others, I'm the Friday regular at Canes', the guy who jaywalked that time, or the kind dude who held the elevator door.

If I die, and this is my last book, which I really hope it's not, I hope you all see me as a good man. A man who loves his family. A man who loves his friends. A man who loves his work and the kind people who pay with their time and hard-earned pennies to see, read, or watch.

If this book could be a summarized in a single sentence, it would be "never kill your inner child". You might be twenty. Thirty. Heck, even sixty-five! But that wonder that gets you excited whenever something you love comes around to greet you, keep it forever.

Now, in their unapologeticly honest and heartbreakingly funny nature, I present to you my Adultish years.

CONTENTS

I. STORIES

II: POEMS

CARLOS LERMA

ADULT*ISH*

I.
STORIES

SORRY, I'M LATE

I 've been metaphorically fearless since the day I was born. When snakes bit me, writing was like sucking out the poison of their bite. Though that doesn't mean the bite scar is not there anymore. I am terrified of sharing my stories with you the same way I would with my best friend, using non-poetic language without metaphors, symbolisms, hyperbole, and pointing out who did what and who said what to me.

When I was younger, I used to be angry at the world, mainly because I did not have many friends. I discovered I could make internet videos that my friends would hopefully find edgy and cool and, therefore, invite me to parties... maybe?

I found camaraderie on the internet, and being a literal child yearning to be heard and seen, that was the perfect storm. That was the pivotal moment in my life that set me on this career path.

I often ponder, had I had more meaningful friendships in my childhood, would I not have sought the approval of strangers for the things I have to say or do on the internet? Would I have followed a different path, like becoming an engineer or app developer, like I once dreamed of as a child? Nonetheless, the internet became where I entered, vented my problems, left, and came back.

It started small and slow. I started by uploading timelapse videos of me painting things like watercolor fish, mountains, and video game characters. Once I got comfortable, that's when things took a turn. I uploaded videos where I ranted about movie ticket prices, people who annoyed me, and a hotel employee on a call. I told these stories as I would to a friend now — jumpy, lots of hand movements, and cursing... a lot of cursing... especially for a 14-year-old. Looking back, everything I did to make a video saddens me.

I used to hope things would go wrong so I could make a video about it. One day, I was on a plane, and a woman with a baby cut in line for the bathroom, and I thought, "Yes, content! Crazy lady is rude to me on a plane?! This will make awesome content!" That's what I worried about as a kid. I hoped things would go wrong so I could run to tell the internet all that happened. I've grown since then, and I recognize that was not healthy.

After growing up a little, I realized all I wanted was to be heard, seen, and be interesting. I felt invisible to my schoolmates, but I did feel liked by my 81 subscribers, who tuned in every week.

After some time, I stopped sharing everything on the internet and realized that some things were just stories for me to keep. After some time, I stopped begging for approval from strangers online.

As a poet, I shared my darkest secrets through funny rhymes. As a filmmaker, I disguised my one-sided friendship as a robot trying to keep a sunflower alive. I depicted meeting my best friend with an exiled monster who finds a firefly in the woods. I confessed my love to someone by turning myself into a ghost, flying away, and haunting them to see them for a night.

These are my secrets, but now they're everybody else's to talk about and discuss.

As a writer, I want to leave a legacy behind. I don't seek to be forgotten while rotten; I'd like that some of the stories that have shaped me into the man I am today to live on, to inspire others, and hopefully, some will learn from my mistakes.

It's taken me a little while to get here. It should've been sooner, but maybe, just maybe, this is the perfect time. So, once again, I apologize for my tardiness.

AMERICAN DREAM

I was alone at my job when I found out I was going to college in America. Every single one of my coworkers had an excuse not to come to work including my boss. I was alone at the office. I applied to a bunch of colleges a few months back. Like every other senior in high school, I've been obsessed with checking my email and admissions portal, waiting for the day my decision comes. This day, was different. It was the one day I didn't check.

I was bored and alone in my office. With no one there, I could order takeout, put my feet on the desk, relax, and maybe call a friend to pass the time. Sometimes, I was done for the day and could go home, but I loved being by myself to think. I like to think by myself a lot.

I completely forgot for a moment that I was waiting for admission decisions. Then, when I realized that I was calm, it hit me, "Oh, this is what I've been stressing about for the past month and a half; let me check if anything changed."

I went over all of the saved tabs on my laptop. I signed in, refreshed, and nothing. That pattern followed up until the last school. For privacy, I will not tell you where I go. If you know, you know.

I opened the last school's admissions portal, and my decision was there. This could go terribly wrong or terribly right, I thought. I clicked the check status, and... I got in. Not only did I get in, but I was also offered a scholarship. I couldn't believe it.

I immediately picked up my stuff from the office, printed the letter, and dashed home. Before driving home at the speed of light, I went to pick my brother up from tennis practice. I picked him up, and when he saw the letter, he couldn't believe it either. I drove home faster than ever because my Dad was leaving the house for his tennis practice after work. I got a hold of him right as he was going to pull out of the garage. I came inside and showed the letter to my parents. They were speechless.

I did it. I wanted to go to America to chase my dreams in entertainment and literature, and this was the start of that. I decided that if I never left, I would never pursue this career path. I would either be a children's therapist, an industrial engineer or work in marketing. The creative/film/book industry is full of uncertainty, and I wanted all or nothing. Go to the big leagues, or nothing. But I got in. This meant that if I once was following my dreams, I would now fall into them.

That meant I was leaving the country in eight months. Those eight months tested me so much, but that's a story for another day, so let's fast forward.

I got to Chicago with four suitcases. Two of them had clothes. One of them had shoes. The last one had my computer, charger, and camera. No posters, no rugs, no lights, nothing. It's cliche, but I came to this country with only a few suitcases and a dream. A dream to be more. A dream to learn. A dream to be a better artist. But part of being a dreamer is being a doer. Now, it was all hands on deck to make that happen.

My Mom, Dad, brother, and uncle dropped me off. It was a bittersweet goodbye, but I visit them every chance I get and call them almost every night. But I was now on my own.

If you know me professionally, you know I love to plan things. Planning releases for films and books is my strong suit.

A few weeks before leaving the country, I met this kid online. We chatted briefly, and I told him I wanted to make a short film as soon as I set foot in the States. He shared the same passion for film as I did, so we got to work as soon as we were both in the city. I did not know then that that he would be one of, if not my, best friend in college.

We winged a six-minute short film titled 'Wish We Never Met.' We had no script, but we did have a bullet-point list. We had no real actors, but I was willing to do it. We had no call sheet, shot list, or natural sense of organization. But, we had the drive to have something made; and that was the thing that made up for everything that was missing. Over two to three weeks, we shot random scenes in random places. But in the end, we weaved everything together into a fantastic short film.

My friend L and I were against all odds and against the world. Since then, we have each been trying to carve a name for ourselves in this world in our respective fields. Since then, we have become much more professional and can't function without a proper shot list and a storyboard.

Him and I got to this country with a fire and drive that will last a lifetime.

INTERNET CHILD

Growing up, I had no hobbies other than drawing and watching TV. Growing up with my little brother, he had such a colorful personality. The dude liked soccer, he liked cool TV shows, and he had friends he hung out with on the weekends. My life up until the third-ish grade consisted of waking up, going to school, coming back, doing my homework, watching TV, going to bed, repeat. I did nothing out of the ordinary for years. Then, my Dad gifted my brother and me a fourth-generation iPod Touch, giving me internet access. Fast forward to sixth grade, I became obsessed with the most incredible American animation show ever to exist called 'Gravity Falls.' After each and every episode came out, I went directly to a guy's channel called Vailskibum (formerly Vailskibum94), where he broke down each episode for the hidden clues and codes that each episode had. I waited for that YouTuber's video about the show with as much anticipation as the actual show he was talking about. Around that same time, I found the channel 'Threadbanger.' It was a channel run by this couple that made YouTube videos about DIY projects on Pinterest; their twist was that they were hilarious and actually did the project, which meant they sometimes failed. Their channel became my comfort zone. I also looked forward to every single one of their videos growing up, and they eventually inspired me to create my own videos centered around the same thing; basically, I'm saying that I wanted to become a carbon copy of Threadbanger.

I started making videos without my face because Vailskibum did videos without his face, so I knew it was not a requirement. What I also left out of my videos when I started out was my actual fucking voice. My videos were just plain time-lapses of me water-coloring things into white cardboard. I kept on doing that for months.

I also failed to mention that ever since I started, I never told my parents any of it. There have been kids in my school who had channels, but my parents did not think it was a good idea for a literal fucking child to be uploading his opinions on the internet; I can now agree with that 100% as I'm writing this in my twenties.

Eventually, I started getting bolder, and I started showing my voice and my face and making videos about personal life stories. My video ritual was waiting for my Mom and Dad to leave the house, then stack boxes from my closet on top of each other, and, at the very top box, to put something for my phone to stand sideways with. I filmed and then edited everything by myself on my phone and laptop. I grew a channel of a little less than 100 subs. I watched Threadbanger so much that I wanted to curse on my videos like they did; each time they did that, I bursted out laughing, so I wanted my audience to do the same. I eventually started cussing, and that somehow made my videos get a little more views. I kept making videos behind my parent's backs for months while my brother knew everything.

My brother then made his own YouTube channel (now deleted), where he uploaded gameplays from whatever video game he played. To the point that one day, we were at the mall, and my brother opened YouTube on one of the display computer models and showed my Dad. While my parents somehow were a bit encouraging of my brother, I still did not tell them about mine, which was a hell of a lot more successful than my brother's. I had 70 subs, he had 10.

One day, before leaving for school, I left my computer open. My Mom was walking by and saw my YouTube channel. The next day, during breakfast, my Mom asked me what this YouTube channel was. I was caught.

My Dad was even more confused because he did not expect me to be the type to upload videos on the internet. My Mom was furious at me because she did not like that I cursed a lot on my channel. When my Dad understood what I was doing, they both demanded that I delete my YouTube channel right before them. My channel had 81 subscribers that morning. With tears and no backup of the videos, I deleted my channel from the internet. After that, I ran to my room and cried; I couldn't believe they'd done this. I worked for months to learn how to edit, film, and build my 81 subs fanbase. Then my Dad came into my room and asked me to understand that if any of the people where he worked found those videos, he could be fired (debatable). He told me he'd allow me to have a new YouTube channel, but they would have to approve everything I uploaded. I agreed and started over. The next day, I pitched an idea for a video to my Mom; she kinda didn't care and just told me to do whatever as long as I didn't curse. After a few months, I eventually started making videos again and regained my 81 subs. After that first pitch, I never went to my parents and asked permission to post something again. To this day, I don't show my parents any films or books before I put them out. Nobody really. I only do it whenever they're about to be out into the world and when it's a little too late to make any changes.

That Saturday morning taught me a precious lesson. First, starting over is okay, especially if you know what you did wrong the first time. Two, take care of your reputation. Because with my old channel, the Moms saw what I was doing and saw me as a bad influence.

Having a YouTube channel gave me an outlet to express myself, and as weird as it sounds, it was good talking to a camera when nobody else really wanted to listen. Strangers on the internet became friends because they liked what I shared. The internet has watched me grow up from 12 years old to my twenties. The internet watched my voice change, become taller, they watched me gain weight, then lose weight, then gain weight again; they watched me put my first film out, then my first book out, and even watched me lose friends. The internet has been a friendly ghost by my side ever since I was a child. And for that, I'll be forever grateful.

The internet taught me how to get a thick skin. I've been told by many people on the internet that I should kill myself, that I'm stupid, and I should stop, but after getting so many, you learn it comes with the job. This one time, I was at a birthday party, and I got a swirl of hate comments from this one live streamer who sent everyone on their live to harass me. It ruined my day; I cried when I got home. As I scrolled on my phone through the hate comments, it dawned on me: this will not be the last time this will happen, so you can either let this destroy you or stand up and keep on.

The internet also taught me how to be a better speaker, holy shit, I spoke by myself to a camera for a BIG part of my pre-teen and teen years. I became less shy and more honest with myself. I became a lot more thoughtful with what I did and said online. I also learned how to be an editor and producer of a web show.

What started as a childhood dream to be a YouTuber morphed into wanting to be a movie director and author. It put me on the path I ultimately needed to be, even if I made some dumb videos.

My advice to anyone starting out is to never stop, keep your head up, and tell your parents what you're doing if you're under 12. Good luck.

GIRLY

I grew up with a lot of women in my life. Really fucking exceptional and role model women. Growing up, I was surrounded mainly (not entirely) by women. I was with my Mom most of the day while my badass Dad was at work (I love you). At school, the guys did not really pay any attention to me (more on that later), and my childhood neighbors were girls, my best friend was a girl, and the cousins I saw the most as a kid were girls. When I grew up, my Mom would take me to brunches with my aunts, and I would listen and sing along to female artists and many little things like that. What I'm trying to say is that I've been impacted and shaped a lot by women.

I don't think every guy in the world can relate to this. Still, to the ones that can, they know how fucking horrible and mortifying it feels to be called girly or gay in elementary school or middle school. I was called girly or gay in middle school regularly. I have mentioned this before, but as a kid, I was very artsy, and still am to this day, and that was one of the things that made me a target for bullies. Whenever I tell stories of situations in elementary or middle school to my high school or college friends, they always tell me how I was bullied, but I never realized. I was never pushed into lockers, some jock never asked me for my lunch money, and no one ever harmed me physically. But I was emotionally fucking destroyed. I still, to this day, convince myself it was not bullying. But it was. I guess.

The fuckers I had as classmates made fun of me for drawing in my little journals, also for not playing sports, or using the popular video game consoles. I went for the plumber video game, and they went for the killing ones (although they high-key grew on me, bet me on COD or GTA, and you will be humbled). On recess, there was this one kid that asked me if I had a penis in front of everyone; after they had their laugh, I went to my girls because they weren't assholes.

If you are a guy and did any of these things to other kids as a kid, just know the guy you did that to will never forget it.

In sixth grade, I started to develop my thick skin. Around that time, I created my YouTube Channel under the name 'DrawTheArt', where I painted something new every week. It could be a watercolor, acrylic, or a sketch. I just liked to draw and paint forever, so I posted that harmless stuff on the internet. I was too afraid to show my face or name, so I hid it. But I slowly made baby steps by starting to talk in my videos, then to start showing my face, and eventually changing my channel name to 'ElCharlieLerma' (TheCharlieLerma). I was known as the artsy kid; everyone said to my face how cool the things I was doing were. Back in sixth grade, having 50 subscribers was the equivalent of being famous. I felt validated by my fucker classmates because I thought that maybe with this, they might like me. Boy, was I wrong.

It was on the last day of sixth grade that I would call my worst day at my elementary/middle school. It was nearing the end of the day, and we were all huddled in a circle in the center of the classroom with all the desks moved so we would fit. We were playing this game where someone asked some generic question like 'Who out of all of us was the funniest this school year?' and everyone would start to vote out loud; the answer was usually unanimous. We played that game for hours with silly questions like 'Who was the smartest?', 'Who was the quietest?', 'Who got into the most trouble?' then, this fucker, who we will call Dick, decides to speak.

Dick asks, 'Who out of here is most likely to be gay?' and everyone bursts into laughter and starts pointing at me while I am frozen. I, out of fucking survival instinct, pointed at a guy I considered my best friend and said, 'No! It's him because he uses pink!' or some ridiculous shit. Everyone then went in a circle and said how and why I was gay. I stood up and went to the bathroom and had a little cry. I looked in the mirror of the bathroom and hated myself. I hated myself because it was something I did not know how to change. I was questioning what it was about me that was indicative of me being gay. They said it's because of how I talk, how I only talk to girls, my taste in stuff.

I talked like this because this is how I've always spoken. I only talked to girls because I have been outcasted from the guys since first grade, and they did not make me feel like shit for being me. I sat in the bathroom with nothing in my thoughts before pretending to brush it off and returning to the classroom.

The aftermath, however, has a happy ending. After years and years, I heard Dick confessed his love to a girl in high school and started crying and sobbing like a bitch in front of her when he got rejected, so there you go, Dick, karma. Also, the kid that then asked me if I had a penis when I was a kid later apologized when we became friends years later when I brought this up one night.

And finally, to the guys who are called girly for being artsy, or for not liking what everyone else wants, or for having a lot of female friends, or whatever it is. Fuck whoever tells you that. You keep drawing and painting, enjoying your tastes, and talking to your gals. No one should have that power over you, let alone some bitch.

THE CHALK THIEF

This story is a testament as to why I can't live without making art, whether it be a drawing, a painting, a poem, a story, a book, a song, or a film. This story happened when I was around five or six years old and takes place in kindergarten.

As a kid, I shared a room with my younger brother; our room was painted red, blue, and white. We had one big desk for two, one TV in front of our two beds, and one single abandoned chalkboard in the corner of the room. That dark green empty chalkboard had always been clean, and there were times I wanted to fill it up with random drawings and musings. My Mom (whom I love; she is the greatest Mom in the universe) knew she had two boys who loved messes, and for that, she did not like to give me access to scissors, tape, paint, chalk, etc. At the time, I saw my mother as this evil monster who did not want the birth of this generation's next big artist. But now, sitting in my college dorm while a pile of dirty dishes is outside my room, I see she was just avoiding possible constant clean-ups, which I totally get now. I'm an adultish man living on my own in another country, and I have to deal with dust, dirty dishes, and fucking vacuuming.

But back to the story, I thought... if my Mom is not going to give me access to chalk for this chalkboard, and I ain't got no dolla dolla bills yo, I thought, where is it that I could steal chalk? Maybe... just maybe... I could steal chalk from my teacher? Boom! Problem solved.

My school was set on two floors; classrooms were on the second floor, and everything else a school has was below; it was a small building, so it made sense. So, at the end of the day, everyone went down. Teachers and students gathered in the school's patio to wait for pickups. When my Mom came to get me, she talked to the teacher quickly, and I pretended to forget a drawing in the classroom. I asked my teacher if I could get it, and she said…YES.

It's about to get an actual spy movie up in this place. I went to the classroom, which had all the lights out. I made my way to the giant classroom chalkboard and found no chalk on the little ledge at the bottom of the chalkboard where all the chalkboard sit. Mission failure. I then remembered the teacher had a big materials box under her desk. So I opened it, and voila, chalk for the taking.

I don't know if this term exists in America. Still, in Mexico, we have a term called "robo hormiga," which translates to "ant robbery." It means that when you want to steal, you first steal little bits that are unnoticeable. So I did that; I took one singular chalk piece out of her dozens and brought it home.

When I came home, I finished that chalk in about thirty minutes; I wiped the board with wet toilet paper time after time from all my different drawings. After some time, my Mom eventually found out I'd been getting chalk from somewhere because the dust on the floor of the room that I always forgot to clean busted my little ass out. I admitted to stealing chalk, and she was lowkey impressed with me doing that, but she also asked me to stop doing it because she and my Dad didn't raise me that way.

The next day, she got me a little box of colored chalk. I was thrilled because all the chalk I stole was white.

THANK YOU, SHANE

Every filmbro on the planet will collectively roll their eyes when I say I did not get interested in filmmaking after one day at the movies, or after watching Star Wars with my Dad, or by being a movie theatre employee. I got inspired by everyday people making films on the Internet. It was on YouTube that I discovered my passion. I had a slight interest in film growing up. Whenever I went into the theater and saw a child actor, I remember always leaving the movie theatre feeling envious of the kid. I felt like I needed to be up there. I felt misbelonging whenever I was a part of the crowd and not the screen. But that little flame of passion approached a gas tank when I discovered the Internet. It was around 2017, and the first short film I ever saw was Shane Dawson's 'The Lottery', I really did not know who he was or what he did, but that short film has been, in my opinion, the best I've ever seen. It's a heartwarming story with a story I related to. Not because I was poor, but because in the story, the kid (the main character) is often made fun of for having feminine traits, and also, the kid had a very, very close relationship with his mother.

After I finished the short film, I felt sad, but I also felt a massive burst of inspiration to do the same thing Shane did. He made a beautiful film about his life without any big studio and only published it on the Internet. So if he could do it, so could I. I binge-watched every short film I could that night to see what the amazing people on the Internet did. I wanted to be like them. I wanted to be a director but in a different way. They told the stories they wanted, how they wanted, without the approval of anybody. I was around 14 years old then and did not want to wait to grow up to try and be a film director. So my impatient ass started right there and then.

Until then, I've been uploading weekly to my YouTube channel, but nothing noteworthy. Just storytimes, advice videos, fun challenges, tags, you know, whatever made a YouTube channel pop off. I stopped making those types of videos and focused on producing original films, which was a very cool transition. A year after I saw Shane's short film, I finally had mine called 'Tragame, Tierra' (Swallow Me, Earth). This experimental short film was just a collection of moments where I wanted to die. Of course, I narrowed it down and excluded the really intense parts, but I kept it honest. I made posters, an excellent thumbnail, and an announcement video promoting my film. When the time came that the film had to be out into the world, I felt like I was finally good at something. Until then, I did not think I was exceptionally good at anything. Anyone can make a Q&A video on YouTube. Still, it takes a particular person to dedicate six months to make an 8-minute short film. The reactions of everyone to the film were overwhelmingly positive, and after that, I knew I could never stop. Since January 25, 2019, my world, my life, has revolved around what film I am doing next, and what inspiration could I use.

I will always have a special place for the Internet because I don't think I would've ever followed my passion without it. And to all my filmbros out there, I'm sorry that my favorite movie is not Pulp Fiction or that I did not get started by seeing my Dad's old movie collection. I've always been kind of an outcast in elementary and middle school, and having a YouTube channel since the sixth grade has always given me a place where I can share stuff when no one in my real life wanted to listen or invite me out on Fridays to play. And for that, I'll never regret being an internet child.

GIRAFFE PLUSHIE

We've all done stupid things for the people we like. Back in eighth grade, I had the biggest crush on this girl. Let's call her Kelly. I thought Kelly was the most perfect girl in the world. She was kind but liked to put people in their place when needed. She wanted to curse as much as I did and was brilliant and clever. At the time, I was drooling over her.

For context, in middle school, my school liked to do these 'Snack Sales' every couple of Fridays where each classroom brought stuff to sell on recess; I'm talking chips, soda, and candy. These are all the things the cafeteria did not give out. The bread and butter of these 'Snack Sales' were the heavenly raffles. Each classroom could stand out based on the things they raffled.

Some classrooms took the easy way out and just brought a couple of gift cards and called it a day. Some others brought toys. Some others didn't even do it. But this time around, the classroom that was raffling stuff was nothing more than genius. This seventh-grade classroom was raffling a gift card, some soap-bubble makers, and a big-ass, fluffy-ass, tall-ass, yellow-ass, cuddly-as-fuck-ass, life-size-ass, 5 feet tall giraffe plushie.

You could buy raffle tickets in recess or whenever kids from the raffle came to the classroom while the teacher was giving a class to ask if anyone wanted to purchase tickets. Later in the day, two kids went into my classroom announcing what they were raffling; Kelly jumped for joy at the sight of the giraffe. The kids asked if anyone wanted to buy raffle tickets; half the classroom did, so we went into the hallway, bought tickets, and returned. Kelly's guy friends (competitors for her heart) all said that if they won the giraffe, they'd give it to her.

I wanted to be that guy. I also said that if I won, I'd give it to her.

Over the day, I came up with this…idea. I went up to the homeroom teacher of the classroom doing the 'Snack Sale' and asked him if he could rig the raffle in my favor so I could win the giraffe. I was really close with this teacher, and he agreed after some convincing. I was now preparing for my moment of romance and heroism.

The raffle winners were announced through the megaphone of the classroom. So everybody would hear when it happened. So, after some waiting, it happened: the megaphone buzzed before letting out the winners. They called the names of all the winners, mine included.

A few minutes later, a kid came into the classroom to hand me my prize. This kid came in asking for me and gave me my beloved prize… I had 'won' the…fucking bubble makers. Not the giraffe. I lost. I mean, I won some shitty colorful bubble makers, but I lost the giraffe.

Kelly was sad she didn't win, and I was frustrated I could've won. I later found out that someone had mixed up the winners' names. I should've gotten the giraffe, but looking back at it now, I'm grateful I didn't get it, as love is so much more than a stuffed animal you give someone. I think the universe needed to teach me the lesson that love can't be forced, and the stars know I've tried.

Since then, I've let things just be.

EX

I don't think I've ever publicly shared any of the relationships I've been in. Back in middle school and high school, I saw how my friends who were couples posted photos to the internet, and everyone cheered for them. Everyone loved them. Everyone envied them. Everyone wanted a "happy" relationship like them. But all would turn around when, one day, their photos on the internet would be deleted without notice, which got people talking, whispering, and, worse of all, inventing. Making up stories. Breaking the relationship even more. They would make the two people that once ended on good terms hate each other for rumors. I never wanted any of that. I've only been in a couple of serious relationships I've never shared with you. Whenever I find the right person, I'll scream their name at the top of my lungs, but for now, I've not met them, and I don't think I will for a while.

But I wanted to talk for a moment about my past romantic relationships because I speak very little of them, even in my poetry and films. I've done movies about longing for love but never about being in love. In my poems, the majority of poetry about fallouts, untrustworthy people, backstabbing, love, belonging, etc., are primarily based on my platonic relationships.

I am one to fall in love with my friends. I care for them so much because I've lost so many over the years. I've lost so many friends I've lost track. I want to address the importance of healing after a breakup with a friend.

Here's a platonic breakup that shook me to my core.

Do you know how, sometimes, one of the people in an ended relationship gets a rebound? That was me in this situation. I was recently kicked out of my middle school friend group, and I was all alone when I entered high school. In Mexico, middle school and high school are significant changes.

Usually, you change institutions entirely, so all your friends from middle school are now dispersed over the city in different high schools.

I had just entered my new high school for the next few years and only longed for one thing. A group of "my boys". I met this one friend, let's call him James. I met James in class, and he introduced me to some of his friends. Eventually, over the following three semesters, we hung out more and more. It all started when James invited me to a party where everyone else from his friend group was there. I was new. They had this group chat named after a dumb *TikToker*. After that, whenever I hung out with them, the way it usually went down was, I would tell James to tell the guys in their group chat to come to my house. Then, I would cook for them and let them drink my alcohol, and every time they came over, I clung to the hope that they would add me to the group chat. It broke me every time they left my house, or I left one of theirs after having a good dinner and talk, and they would still not add me to the damn group chat. I mean, how fucking hard is it?

It was until one day, after a cookout in my house, that they added me. It felt like I was a dog, and after crying to the people living in a house I found, they let me in. And boy, did they let me in. They let in all the inside jokes, the secrets, the hangouts, and most of all, a group of boys I longed for since I was kicked out of my last friend group by vote…on Christmas. Needless to say, I was so scarred by my last friend group that I wanted to keep this one at all costs.

Eventually, I started noticing things I didn't like. There was this one kid, let's call him David. David was the butt of every joke in the group. He was made fun of because of his taste in music, clothes, crushes, and past attempts at relationships. However, he drove them around, invited them to his house more than mine, and paid for things they would use or eat. They used this kid to their advantage, but he didn't know. I saw how he was so angry at these guys for making fun of him, but he, like I, was scared to lose them, so he kept going.

Also, as time passed, the 13-person group had inside beef and smaller friend groups. Friends made out with other friends' exes or crushes and violated the bro code. And guys that lived close gathered without telling the rest of the guys, but they were the main guys, so no one, including me, could give them shit.

I told them I got into film school. They cheered. But things came afterwards. One of the saddest things I've heard came after telling them. The first one is that James confided in me that he always wanted to pursue fashion. He's a stereotypical straight dude with a very old-fashioned family, so he told me he would never chase it, but nonetheless, it was the thing he loved. After months, he started teasing me, telling me I should go down an actual path in life, making jokes about how studying "movies" meant that every time I went to the movies, I just studied the consistency of popcorn. They were very clearly insults. One day, a few weeks before I left Monterrey for Chicago, I confronted him about it, and he attempted to gaslight me into saying he's my number one fan. I just was tired of them at this point. A few days later, I found out they'd been secretly waiting for me to leave the country to kick me out of the group chat. Mind you, I've never been anything but kind and loving to these ungrateful motherfuckers.

I found that out three days before my farewell party for college. Three fucking days. I would leave the country in five. I debated to uninvite them because I was so angry and heartbroken that I did not want to see them before leaving. A friend finally talked some sense into me and told me to just let them come and let them go, and I did. They came to my party. And four days later, I left.

When I was now in Chicago, I was just waiting for them to kick me out of the group chat out of the blue. But...that never happened. Instead, I talked once a month in that group chat. I had some decent conversations with people from that group chat outside of it. Everything was fine.

When I returned home that same year for winter break, things took a turn. Since they all hung out in smaller groups before I left, I did the same and thought nothing of it. I decided to invite my three closest friends from that group to dinner. We had a blast and talked as if not a day passed. I took some photos and posted them online, and the other guys in the friend group eventually saw them.

One of the "main" guys screenshotted it and sent it in the group chat the very next day; let's call this douchebag, Ass. Ass said, "Kick him out already," and proceeded to kick me out of the group chat and not say a word. What surprised me was that there was only one person who not only defended me but also talked to me about it. And that's my hometown best friend, which I love wholeheartedly. I would not be alive without him. Other than him, no one reached out, not even to fight or see what was wrong. I accepted my fate and just kept living. That same day, I went to the movies to see M3GAN. During the movie, I was mad. Not mad because they kicked me out, but because I was sure Ass was feeling like he was so right for doing what he did. It was a they left me before I left them scenario. In my mind, and I'm sure theirs too, they won. In one day, I metaphorically lost eleven friends. Since that day, I've not talked to them other than just three. And I really don't plan on changing that anytime soon. I don't want forgiveness or peace; I want nothing from them.

I want to point out that when Ass sent the photo and kicked me out I was the only one kicked out of the four in the picture. He was looking for an excuse to kick me out, and he got it. But the one thing he did not get was a plea for me to stay. I've learned in the last twenty years that when people want you around, they'll let you know, and when they don't, they'll tell you, too.

To this day, I don't know what I did to them to make them hate me. I've always been kind, loyal, supportive, and honest to them. That day, I got kicked out but it felt like I had let go of an anchor on my back I had been carrying since the few days before my farewell party.

I lost friends, but I found out that the problem was them.

DAD

My Dad has one of the most robust work ethics I've ever seen in a person. Ever. I'm sure every CEO worldwide could learn a lot from my Dad. He is the absolute fucking best. Since I was a child, he also instilled in me a solid work ethic. As a kid, he saw I was artsy; like any father, he had his doubts about where art could take me, but he then shrugged it off and told me: "I'll let you be whatever you want in this world, with one condition: you must be the best." He didn't mean it when he said, "I'll let you," but you get the sentiment. He reminded me often whenever we talked about my career that he wanted me to give my 200% in everything I do. He also taught me to avoid the word "but." He told me that whenever his colleagues say "but" to him, he already knows that what follows after that word is a useless excuse. He taught me many more things, but I'll keep those secrets, ours.

My Dad is a businessman, a good man, and a father. Up until a year or two ago, I did not recognize that as I do now, mainly because I was a teenage dirtbag that had other priorities and a shittier out view on life, but there was a moment when that all changed.

My Dad has had many endeavors throughout his life. When I was a kid, he mainly ran marathons. He ran five Major Marathons: Chicago, New York, Tokyo, Berlin, and London. He never qualified for the Boston Marathon. He eventually stopped running and lived a pretty ordinary life. He also tried other endeavors like guitar. He just wanted to use his time for something fun. I don't know how or exactly when, but he got into tennis about a year ago.

Whenever he picked up a new endeavor, he always bought everything he needed. If he was running, he purchased the shoes, the gear, the glasses. If he was playing guitar, he bought the quality guitar, the picks, the case. With tennis, he purchased all the necessary things.

My Dad started training and loved it. He eventually got his very first match. He lost. Then he got another one. And lost again. He played so many matches over a month or two and lost every single one. But the thing that made me open my eyes to who the fuck my Dad was, was that he never quit. Never. Sure, he got home a little bummed out, but he picked himself up as fast as he had fallen. He stood stronger and ready to face the challenge again. One night, he said, "If I lose this next match I'll know then it's time for me to leave tennis behind."

He won that night.

I felt so proud of him; I thought I could do anything.

Throughout my life, he has taught me that life will knock you the fuck down many, many times. But if there's one thing he taught me, you should never give up. Even if you have no backup. Even if you've lost a thousand times. Even if the crowd laughs at you. Even if you lose to someone younger or older. Never quit.

A month ago in April, years after his last marathon, he finished the Boston Marathon. My Dad never quit. He just took a little breather. Also, he got knee surgery, but he said fuck that. How badass is that? I have the coolest Dad in the world.

FREEDOM

I made my Dad worried sick on the first day of first grade when I was a child. I remember that day perfectly. The grade before first grade, whatever grade that may be for you, the way pick-ups went was your Mom or Dad came and got you on the car pickup line. A teacher would use a radio to tell another teacher that your parents were there, and they would then hold your hand all the way up to the car.

But first grade was different. Being a first grader meant that all school grounds were up for exploration. The soccer field, the patio, the bleachers, the cafeteria. Everything. Since my Dad was not used to that routine, he asked me to meet him at a place in the school. I forgot, and to this very day, I forgot where in the school he wanted me to stand to wait until his arrival.

Nonetheless, as soon as school ended, I roamed the school from top to bottom. I halted my expedition when I encountered a sale for icy pops, a lemon icy pop; it was necessary.

Time flew, hours passed, and I totally forgot about my Dad. My Dad, while I was having a fucking blast, was calling the school, worried sick about where the fuck his child was and how the school could lose a child. Teachers told my Dad they did not know where I was. Nonetheless, he eventually found me with my lemon icy pop in hand. He was angry, to say the least. When I got home, my Dad yelled at me for good reason. He imagined the worst.

Fast forward a decade and a half, and I'm living in another country. My parents have always been present. I love them. They've never left my side; I now talk to them daily. Whether that be a phone call, a video call, a single message, or a meme, I speak to them. To an angsty teen, you might think, "Ugh, Mom, stop bothering me." but now, as an adult, I'm grateful my parents are very much present in my life. When I moved to Chicago about a year ago, I remembered the icy pop incident; I realized about two nights after my parents dropped me off that they had given me the freedom every teenager wanted.

If you had asked me when I was 15, what would I want to do if I lived alone? I needed to figure out where to start, but it would not have been responsible.

After a few days in the city, I wanted to do something cool and alone. So I bought a ticket to a show by an indie singer. I used to live around Harrison Station on the Red Line in my first year of college, and the concert I wanted to go to was all the way to Lincoln Park. When I saw the distance, I was scared. Scared to get robbed. Scared to get lost. Afraid of the night, honestly. But I knew that I was an adult now. I know my Mom and Dad would generally tell me to take a friend or that she could take me, and if those options were not possible, then I wouldn't go. But I wanted to do this for myself as a moment to recognize and celebrate the giant leap I took moving out of my home and also of my country. I had a taste of independence. No curfew, no rules. I sang my heart out at that concert and came back home safely.

There is a time for everything.

A time when you want to run away because your Mom or Dad did not let you go to the movies. A time when you get your first car. The time when you have sex for the first time. The time to get your first job.

Throughout my life, I've been getting more freedom, but I'm grateful I've gotten that freedom when I'm mentally prepared to take on that freedom. Since that icy pop incident, my parents have unlocked parts of life for me at just the right time, and for that, I'll be forever grateful because it prevented me of making huge mistakes.

Instead of spending my dollars at the mall and the movies, I save them, buy better groceries, save for a good dinner with friends, go to the zoo, or save them on personal and passion projects.

More freedom doesn't always mean more problems. You just need to be a little adultish for the following freedom. Except for alcohol, at the time of my writing this, I am 20. It's insane I have to wait another year to drink legally here in America.

WORKAHOLIC

I'm afraid I won't find a job after I graduate. It haunts me daily. It torments me. It occupies my every second of every day because I see it everywhere. I see it whenever my friends advance in their careers. Whenever I step into my dorm. Whenever I go to class. I'm terrified that whenever I die, all I've done will dissolve into nothingness in everyone's memory.

In college, I've developed less-than-ideal habits.

In March 2023, I started going to bed at least at four in the morning. I was in a relationship then, and as much as I wanted to give my all to the relationship, I was worried about keeping up with my work. Obviously, I always put my relationship first. So, whenever my girlfriend came to my apartment to sleep, I'd wait for her to fall asleep after spending time together, and I'd work the hours away at night. I'd be writing, editing, or making progress in whatever little thing I could. I pulled an insane number of all-nighters while animating 'Firefly.' I'm the type of person who can not continue living knowing that some work could be done, some progress, and some extra steps to take. I feel anxious to leave something unfinished. So, I would not sleep until that happened.

I remember the very first time I pulled an all-nighter. I was editing my short film "The Wright Choice." "The Wright Choice" was actually a school project. For context, we made a short film centered around two characters, one location, and all under 5 minutes. The 8-minute film cut included all the extra scenes I shot that I did not have in the assignment.

Nonetheless, two friends and I got together many nights to make progress. Each night, we got closer to our goal. We all decided to not leave the study room until we finished. And so, we did. The film was done by the time the sun came up.

I got to class, dead inside. I could not focus, I could not stand straight, I could not function. I've never pulled an all-nighter, so to my body, all these things were new.

As we were all screening our films to the professor, the professor looked at me and asked if I was sick or felt okay; I assured him I was not and asked to go home. By that point, it was noon. I got home and woke up at 7PM. I thought I'd never do this again, but I've done it countless times after that.

During my second semester in college, I lost track of the time I started working at 11P.M., then looked out the window, and the sun was already out. At that point, I'd go to bed and wake up after 2PM.

My nutrition got worse. I stopped having breakfast altogether. Times when I woke up and made myself a pretty neat breakfast made of two eggs with ham or bacon, orange juice, and toast, were gone. I'd wake up just in time to shower, go to class, and eat later if I had time.

I am a workaholic.

When I was little, I listened to the adults saying the words: "alcoholic" or "foodaholic." I've heard those and many other words, but when it came to the word "workaholic," I thought, how can it be wrong to be addicted to something that gives you money? I returned to the phrase, "If you love what you do, you'll never work a day in your life." I applied it to my life. I looked at my desk filled with hard drives, cables, and SD cards and thought: I love this life. I love making these films, animations, and books. Whenever I sit down and do things like this, time flies by. But "workaholism," like all isms, is terrible.

My Mom taught me very young that everything in extreme amounts is terrible. Excessive amounts of love are harmful. Excessive amount of vegetables is bad. Excessive amounts of exercise are bad. Excessive amounts of work is awful.

What I've been doing to my body in the past months has been putting it through every test. I've lost sleep, I've gained weight. And I try and justify it with, "It's gonna be worth it if it's for my future!"

I'm still, to this day, a workaholic. As I write this, I still am. But now I'm actively trying to stop. To get sleep. To eat breakfast. I know now that the desperation to make it this young and this early will take me to unhealthy places.

However, the fear I'll not make it will haunt me until I do. I just need to battle my demons.

88

BETTER LATE, THAN NEVER

S o until we meet again in book form, this, for me, is yet another goodbye for now. The tales I just shared with you, dear friend, are the experiences that have shaped me into the adultish man I am today.

Now, it's time to grow and to keep living.

Right now, I'm living in the anxiety of uncertainty. I'm in my sophomore year in college, and that brings a whole other set of challenges to overcome. Ultimately, I always want to make my parents proud, my friends proud, and you: proud, entertained, and inspired. Over the last months I've been living alone in this country, I've learned to fight for myself because if I don't, then who will?

Leaving my parent's home was the single most important lesson of them all. To clean my room, do laundry, pick up after myself, and cook for myself. We despise doing these things as kids but despise not doing them as adults because if we avoid those things, life can become overwhelming.

Love is still something I've not found. But I'll find someday; if not, so be it.

Friendship is more than hangouts at the mall. It's understanding each other, being far and still being in touch, loving each other in the way that you accept their flaws and choose to enjoy their company. Friendship is sitting alone in silence in the living room; friendship is crying drunk; friendship is telling each other when you're wrong; friendship is everything.

My career is challenging; I'm trying to be a recovering workaholic; I try to put my mind in other places that are not my work. But only time will tell if I'm successful. I need to learn that good things will come, and it will be worth it when they do. The late-night writing, the early morning commuting, the rejections, and everything that came after chasing a dream will ultimately be worth it.

Now you know me a little better, don't you? I apologize for being late, but hey, better late than never, huh?

Now, I've got some more secrets to tell you.

II.
POEMS

HE WROTE IT ABOUT YOU?

I am writing you a love letter today,
because of all my hate from yesterday
poisoned my roots, making them rot.

I've been exiled and tossed,
like a toy with no cost,
living as someone I'm not.

I'll write to those who ran and hid
and mail this goodbye in the wind.

To the friend who was silent—
who sold nothing for gold,
with a fool as a client,
to a warning so common and old.

To my bad blood fellows—
whose voices still echo
in my mind's growing hell hole.

I built a ladder with nothing more
than my puny flesh and bones,
but came out stronger, I suppose.

To my dead old self —
I'll bring flowers to your grave
but will never return I'm afraid.

ADULTISH

I'm afraid I lost my teenage years
chasing after adulthood dreams.
I'm afraid I lost time and friends
to poetry and films.

I drew, wrote, and painted
alone in my childhood bed.
I ran after dreams as a kid
until my legs were as good as dead.

I've worked endless hours
for love, joy, and money,
but after endless days
that dream seems farther away.

I chased the rainbow
for promised treasure
only to find it was never there.

All I wanted was to make art
for the rest of my life
for whomever might care.

My underdog days are over,
summer turned to autumn,
and I'm standing here thinking:
When did I grow up?

AGAIN, AGAIN!

What a shitty streak
with months to weeks
waiting like a freak
with four different clicks,
treating each as mystique,
with every try a new tweak.
The outcome bleak
though that made me shreak,
and also feel oddly unique.
I knew I was my own clique
when I ceased to seek.

Anyways,
again, again!

CAN'T KILL ME, BABY

Your frown is so cartoonishly perfect,
'cause every time you say I'm not worth it,
your bullet goes right through me
without ever hurting my organs.

So, now, you gotta pull up your arsenal,
Every other weapon used before now isn't as functional.

I think, "Hah, bitch!"
Your sword lost its edge.
Oh! — And what's better revenge
than to live after all that bleeding?

I say, "Hah, bitch!"
You just know no bounds.
Why? 'Cause every single time
I move on, and you try to drag me with you.

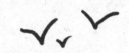

No — I'm not falling for it again,
I was walking distracted and fell,
fell in love, and now we bid our farewells.

So, I now look down whenever I walk
'cause living a cautious life is better.

Now my smirk is so cartoonishly perfect,
'cause all the old tricks are not even working.
You're a sinking ship, and I am your ocean.
Ahoy, my friend! Your downfall will be my slogan.

I SHOULDN'T HAVE DRANK

My heart was empty,
like the bottles on the floor.
My bladder was full,
like the party from before.

I asked to use the toilet and
forgot to go as soon as she opened
the door to the apartment we entered so slowly.

My brain, after hours complained
that my bladder never got drained,
so I ran to pee and asked myself
what situation I was now in.

Sitting on the sidewalk alone, heartbroken,
I think I could've held it in.

YOUR POWER

No enemy could betray me—
as no foe ever held the power
to tear my heart to pieces,
only a friendly blade running free
could show you the disaster
that the lesson teaches.

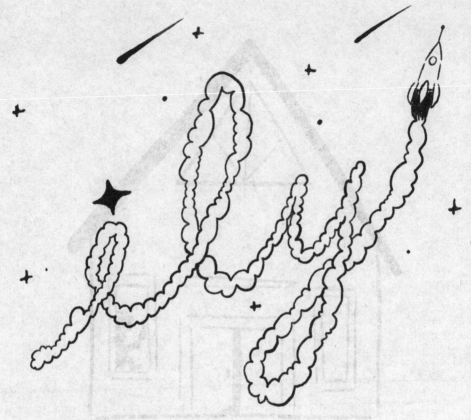

ASTRONAUT

I used to hop from planet to planet
looking for a home.
I sailed all the uncharted waters
looking to halt my roam.

You're not a place,
but nonetheless,
I feel protected.

Now not displaced,
I must confess,
I love you.

ARE YOU GAY?

It's a lifelong mystery
that everybody wants to know.

It's a battle with myself,
yet the world is involved.
It's like I'm hiding a body,
and there's a crime to be solved.

They theorize like I'm a conspiracy
and analyze my speech patterns
like it's some sort of mystery.

They speak as if they have no doubt
but if I answer, I'd be giving something
for all the people to talk about.

I'll be myself, but at what cost?
They don't know, so they all guess
if I'm gay, bi, pan, or something else.

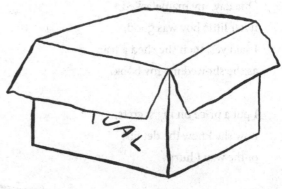

MY SON'S A WRITER

I was sad at school,
I was a weird kid.
When I wanted to play,
all the boys ran and hid.

I wanted to tell a soul,
but people were in other places.
So, I'll tell my secrets
to empty college-ruled pages.

I'll make my journals my buddies,
because it feels like it's somebody
who will always be there.

I stumbled with my studies,
to try and make money,
off a book I made.

It was late October,
what I wrote got exposure.
It was now in paperback,
all my teenage disclosures.

One day, my mama asked,
if her little boy was good,
I said yes, then she shed a tear,
as she showed me my book.

I put a price on my secrets,
now she knew the details,
of the way I hurt.

No way to go back and reset,
all that was done and said
long ago, now a blur.

She was broken she didn't notice.
She and my Dad pleaded, "Next time, tell us."
I said, "You now got no reason to be afraid."
I had bad moments that now get me paid.

She thought it was her fault,
but I assured she was wrong.
My parents were concerned
and even thought they made mistakes.

I explained to them they had raised someone
kind and loving, but hard to break.

I'm sorry I gave you a scare then,
I promise you it won't happen again.
I healed the sad stuff I wrote in pen,
Now I'm emotionally an eight out of ten.

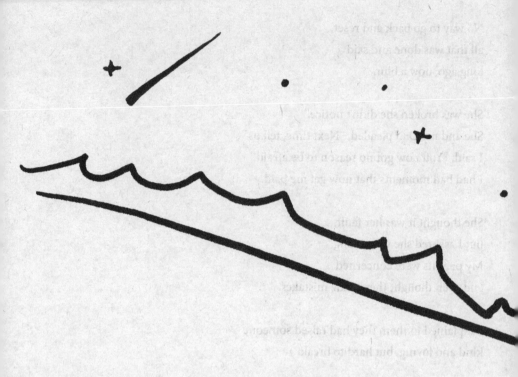

GONE, GONE, GONE

The power bestowed
upon the knight in shining denim.
Then came the sorrow,
as silence filled me with its venom.

A flight—close to the sun—
came to an abrupt end
in the morning.

The knight was now gone,
a quiet goodbye to a friend
without warning.

MERCURY HEART

My little mercury heart
is cold and gray and lonely.
It looks out the window
for someone to hold it very closely.

However, not anyone would do,
as everybody's ice-cold, too.

This world has
cold walls, cold floor, cold seats
but very few flames
walking out on these streets.

I look for the one who will melt me
at the very first sight and touch.
I feel like I'm not asking for much.

Guess what, I'm doomed!
I found a flame!
At this lame-ass party
but I need to know their name.

My little mercury heart
takes no more guests.
But for you, I'd evict everybody
from my heartbreak hotel.

I stutter, you laugh, I smile
my heart's on my face.
Kinda wished you asked me
to get outta this place.

We got chemistry,
you took my breath away.
Well, of course,
fire consumes all oxygen.

My little mercury heart
melted at the sight of the most divine.
And revealed that all that mercury
was just armor all this time.

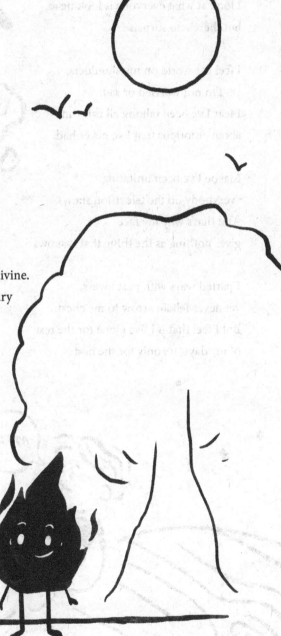

I FEEL FUCKING NOTHING

I look at everyone, look at everything
with stars in their eyes.
I look at what everyone is looking at,
but there's no surprise.

I feel the world on my shoulders,
yet I'm not worried or sad.
I fear I've been talking all this time
about emotions that I've never had.

Maybe I've been imitating
everybody on the television shows.
And that's why my face
gives nothing as the thing that it shows.

I parted ways with past lovers,
yet never felt an arrow to my chest.
But I feel that if I live alone for the rest
of my days, it's only for the best.

They all ask if I feel something,
but what the heck should I know?
I barely know this language;
I might as well go.

I don't look at the trees,
the birds or the fucking bees.
The sound of my jingling keys
bring nothing but nothing to me.

I might have a factory error.
Does it really get better?
Is this forever?
I can't stand this pressure to feel something, anything.

CONFIDENTIAL

▇▇▇▇▇▇▇▇▇▇▇▇▇▇▇▇▇ I don't sing to the world ▇▇▇▇▇▇

▇▇▇▇▇▇▇▇ all about my lover ▇▇▇▇▇▇▇▇▇▇▇▇▇▇▇▇

▇▇▇▇▇▇ for fear the ▇▇▇▇▇▇▇▇▇▇▇▇▇ world breaking us,

and all will be over. ▇▇▇▇▇▇▇▇▇▇▇▇▇▇▇

▇▇▇▇▇ I hid it out of ▇▇▇▇▇▇▇▇▇▇▇▇▇▇▇▇ privacy,

you ▇▇▇▇▇▇▇▇ hid it out ▇▇▇▇▇▇▇ of shame.

LIGHTNING IN A BOTTLE

Tears for men come around like
lightning in a bottle.
Scared men ought to laugh and say
"That's the worst role model"!

"CLOWNS"

You and I defy everybody
and also shun vocabulary.

We see each other,
yet don't hold hands.
I pay for your meal
as if it's the plan.

We meet up
and sit on my bed.
But we're each
on opposite ends.

You and I miss each other
and get upset,
if one doesn't text.

I gift you my time and love
and what's worse is
you do the same.

I try to be brave
but daydream of
us sharing a house, bed,
and even last names.

We're fearless but scared.
I hope that's the reason for your silence.

It's not that we're afraid
to take this to the next stage.
It's simply that there's no word
for what you and I have made.

FOOL

When butterflies come around
in your stomach's little town
sip some water,
and watch the fuckers drown!

UGLY EX-BOYFRIEND

I made her cry just the other night,
because all her friends asked,
"Is that really your man"?

I look at the foggy mirror's sight
and I hate what I see.

You projected onto me like a movie screen,
blinding light, and I was a dumb fly.
I get your intentions were never to be mean,
it's just that I'm not as hot as all the other guys.

It's somehow my fault I'm not hot,
and you justify it to hide the shame.
Your friends grab and gut your heart,
and somehow I'm the one to blame.

I want to walk away,
But all I want is to try again.
I grab a new jacket,
one that does the trick just right.

Months pass, I cut all ties,
and try to recalibrate my eyes.

I guess of all the guys you got over,
I'll just be your ugly ex-boyfriend.

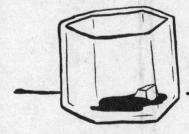

LOVE ON THE ROCKS

Love is your favorite drink.
Lonely sobers don't understand.
The world is your favorite bar,
full of people, choices, and demand.

They might be everything for a night
drunk, calling each other lovers
until they sober up and realize
they need something stronger.

You'll go meet every drink
at this bar called "earth"
until you find the one
that will always be that strong.

MADE IN MEXICO SMILE

You know I love you way way more.
I adore your new-to-me American style.
It's like I'm a candy-starved child,
asked for gum, then got the whole damn store.

You like my made-in-Mexico smile,
compliment my simple-guy style,
and enjoy all I do and say.

I appreciate the jokes only you and I get;
don't forget, it's you and me against the world.
We might come from faraway places,
but I don't want to leave the prettiest person I've observed.

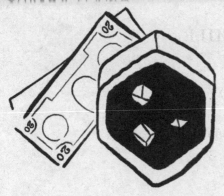

KISS ME, KISS ME, LOVE

Who do you think you are?
You're the hottest person in this bar.
I know you're smart, but we will get there soon.
I'm not thinkin' straight; it feels like ages passed, but it's only June.

Who do you think I am?
I'm the coldest heart across the land.
You lit a match, yet all my ice came falling down.
Not thinkin' straight, I just know you saved me from being drowned.

So, I have just one request,
I don't know if you can tell
what my hands and eyes suggest.
So, I'll just ask and hope for the best.

Kiss me, kiss me, love.
Make me choose where,
and I'll circle "all of the above."
You better leave no stone unturned.

Kiss me, kiss me, love.
Make me choose when
and I'll run to you right now,
I'll be so fast the world spins the other way around.

Kiss me, kiss me, love.
Make me answer why,
I'll say I've waited for the longest time,
even though it feels like the biggest crime.

Kiss me, kiss me, love.
Make me answer what?
What are we? We are everything,
we could be lovers until you get bored of me.

Kiss me, kiss me, love.
Make me choose who,
and you know I'll choose you every day,
I hope you choose the boy from Monterrey.

So, kiss me, kiss me, now.

MARTINI FANTASY

There's something I wanna say to you,
but I'm afraid I'm too afraid.
I had it in my head, but you had no clue,
when we drove just the other day.

I'm not on the list of people that you've kissed,
it's like you think the chance doesn't exist.
So all I'll do with you, I guess, is just resist.
For leaving you unkissed leaves me pissed.
But only at myself.

You said, "Let's go somewhere else."
I thought, "This is finally my chance."

So, inside my car we went,
it was hot, but the ice didn't melt.
No moves, it was like I was dead.

If I could, I'd steal you like a jewel,
but I don't have much time left in this town.
But with me gone, I'd lose the duel,
so I'll cherish what I can get before I'm gone.

I'll pine away every night,
and hold the fairfarren gift very tight,
until I can fall asleep tonight.

I hugged my pillow pretending it was you,
I'm glad no one has you, but it still hurts.
I told myself I would tell you before I left,
but the butterflies ate away my guts.

I'm a country away from you now,
but I still hold you with bliss,
hoping that all I'll get when I'm back,
is just a long-awaited kiss.

My dear old friend, I'm back in town,
a year has passed since you've been to where I live,
we catch up like no time has passed,
but midnight comes, and you have to leave.

I closed the front door,
and I didn't feel it again.
The feeling wasn't as strong
as it was way back when.

The beverage I once chased,
which was your beautiful face,
has now lost it's aftertaste
of thinking of you all day.

You never broke my heart,
it's weird, I'll explain.
I must confess that,
you broke my brain.

You feel different, but you're still there.
I lost all feelings for you in a moment,
now my heart has mind room to spare.

I'm back in Chicago, but this time
I walk down Clark Street feeling just fine.
After coming down the mountain I just climbed,
patched little heart but I'm alright.

I kept things like pens and rocks
to remind me of you.
But now they're in a shoe box,
that became their tomb.

I took a shot, and then I took three,
the martini shot, of our fake love movie,
was us driving as friends,
and that's all we'll ever be.

It'll be my 'martini fantasy',
the very, very last fake scenario,
I'll think about before I let you go.

What we never had,
may now rest in peace.
For my sake, I'll just imagine
we had a goodbye kiss.

HOUSEFIRE

You hid your matches,
when all my garden burned.
Because every foe I've got
was a friend on day one.

I regret and rue the day
I took off my armor.
I was your friend
now I'm your karma.

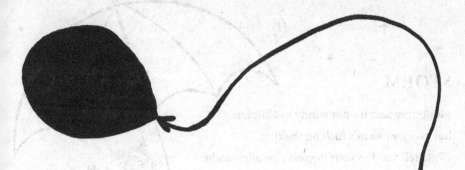

PORCUPINE

We could smoke and talk until the sunrise,
or laugh until one of us dies.
I did not know what this was before.

Our paths are strange, but nonetheless,
I feel like after these days, I must confess
that the universe finally answered my call.

I feel time's been irrelevant,
as we are so different yet similar,
in a way no one else can understand.

If I could count all my people
from being born till today,
you would be the first finger lifted from my hand.

However, I know you can never be mine.
So, I'll mourn what I never had all June,
alone in my bedroom like a porcupine,
who was stupid enough to love a balloon.

And I'll live the rest of my days hurting,
cursing the universe for doing me dirty.

STORM

Monterrey said it's not windy in Chicago,
but every window's fucking shaking.
Gotta tell you I'm your biggest new aficionado:
we could be more than friends in the making.

Makes me wanna go outside
to hold up an umbrella:
want to use the wind to
fly with me forever?

The weather ain't pretty
right here in this city.
It ain't that shitty, really.

When you came around
all was getting bad,
the city blew around
and put you right beside me.

You came then stayed,
afraid you'll walk away
leaving me here strayed.
How can I put this in writing?

This city's strong breeze
calmed all my pleas
because it gave me you.

FAIR FIGHTS AREN'T FAIR

I brought my words to a gunfight.
Because my syllables put together shoot to kill.
I might end up bruised, but never killed.
You did it to destroy me, I did it for the thrill.

You say actions speak louder than words,
but baby, you couldn't be more wrong.
For them can infest your body like worms,
or stay stuck in your mind like a pretty song.

I don't talk to please, or to cause debate.
I just want to set the record straight.

I MISS YOU

If nightmares were the only way,
I'd be able to see your daydream face,
I could die happy knowing you are out there,
living far on your little corner of the earth.

POISON IVY

They say the grass is greener on the other side.
But what if everybody's colorblind?
I have my little garden in my little house.
Why pay anyone else's any mind?

Passing neighbors
throw dirt, others flowers
dirt-throwers scream, but they're all cowards.

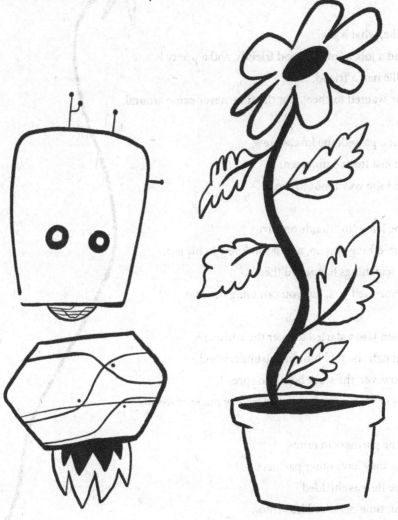

INFIDELITY STORY

Jason was eighteen,
we had a little friend group, and I was there.
Jason had a girl,
she was everything, but he was a nothing boy.

He said, our fire would never die.
But the light from their so-called love
was coming from the end string of a dynamite.

Ellie, what a gal,
had a job, a "man," good friends, and a pretty house.
Ellie had a friend,
she wanted to cheat, but the time never came around.

Time passed, the lovers grew,
he just turned nineteen,
and she was about to too.

She left with friends on a trip.
Something was up, and Jason knew in his gut.
A few things happened then,
I won't tell you, but you can imagine what.

Then Jason started to hear the whispers,
though she told him he misunderstood.
However, the story began to spread,
faster than a fire in a paper factory made of wood.

True partners in crime,
but they have other partners.
The lie was shielded
but, time dissolved it's armor.

Jason now heard it all,
from the beginning to the very end.
Leaving out all doubts,
but the fool didn't believe his only friend.

The town knew her name,
but the rumor disturbed her tranquility.
Everybody gossiped
how she finished summer with an infidelity.

To this day,
Jason still believes Ellie's a saint.
To this day,
Jason believes everything is going great.

You might be wonderin' why I didn't spill.
It's because good ol' Jason crossed yours truly.
She got away with murder, but nobody knows.
Except, of course, all of you, my dear reading fellows.

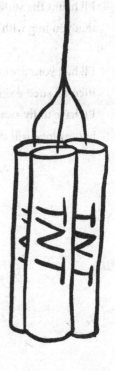

CLARK STREET GHOST

I live alone on Clark Street,
thousands of miles away.
I try to find someone here
who understands me the same way.

When I miss you,
I dream of something special.
Something that has
the magic potential
of having my ghost
travel home to you.

My eyes glow white,
I go to sleep in time,
for my ghost to roam tonight.

I'll haunt the stuffed bear
that you hug with loving care.

I'll hug your arm with my body,
then I'll shed a single tear.
I'll have to fly away by sunrise,
but my love will stay here.

LAST YEAR'S SUMMER

A plane took me to my hometown.
What would follow?
Tacos Primo and old friends
took my mind off Chicago.

I'm in the best bar downtown,
it's been a little while.
Dancing to songs they would never get,
getting a little wild.

My old friends came close
and asked, "How's the city, ain't it cold?"
I smiled and responded,
"It's kinda whatever but it never gets old."

I talked with my best friend for hours,
the hugs were tight while we were both high on life.
We talked about the past and the present,
and through old enemies' neighborhoods took a drive.

Who knows if I never left
what could've been?
There's a chance my future
could've died on the scene.

Chicago sent winds as whispers,
telling me "I miss you, please come back."
I felt them come through the mountains,
while on my balcony having a snack.

I enjoyed Monterrey while it lasted,
hugged and kissed my father and mother,
then came back after enough time passed.

CHANCES

If my candles had water as light
and my eyes bled fire and sparks,
would my heart be stone instead of flesh?

What if you saw me like I see you,
and I ignored every signal you sent?
Do I really wanna pass on the lament?

You saw a side of me.
I've hidden for ages.
Now, all I have to show for it
are all of these pages.

Why won't you dare to jump
and give this one single try?
Where do I go to bury
this heavy load of heartbreak supply?

For the sun will rise at night.
The day you might give me a chance.

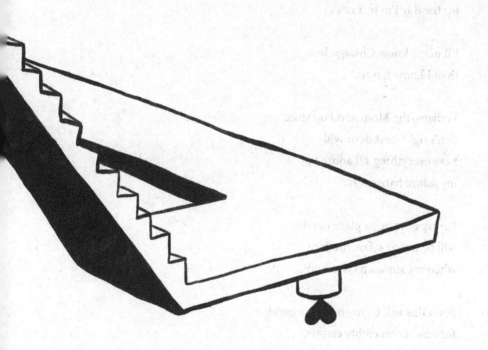

CLARK STREET?

I was walking down Clark Street
instead of going home—
my new home, my American home.

A home without furniture
a home without memories.

I know exactly where I am,
but I'm lost.

I don't know these streets,
I don't know these shops,
I don't know the shortcuts
for the day I'm in a rush.

I'll never know Chicago less,
than I know it now.

Perhaps, the Mom and Pop store
that's right next door will
have everything I'll adore for
my future hangovers.

Perhaps the pizza place nearby
will be my new favorite spot
when my stomach's in a knot.

Soon this will be my neighborhood:
for now it's an empty canvas,
to which I have the paint.

S Clark St

LETTERS TO STRANGERS

Dear B,

I'm truly sorry I bullied you in first grade. Thanks for returning the favor a decade later.

Dear Dick,

Fuck you for what you did to me in sixth grade. It fucked me mentally to this day. (Mentioned in "Girly")

Dear D,

We're friends now, but we weren't for a minute. I will always have my questions as to why we went from brothers to strangers in a day. Also, sorry I never said hi to you at parties, that was weird. You are a talented artist and I hope you find happiness.

To Whom It May Concern,

I had a crush on you but never admitted it. I love(d) you.

Dear R,

Sorry for breaking up with you at school. I think we would've lasted longer had your parents not being strict. Sorry to have blamed it on you. You're truly wonderful and talented. I hope you're happy with whoever you end up. Also, you never answered my text when I asked to get coffee. I'm still down to catch up after all these years.

Dear S,

You broke my camera and never paid me back. Also, I don't know if you had a crush on me...kinda seemed like it. Anyways, pay me back.

Dear M,

Thanks for friendzoning me, we work much better as friends.

Dear Friend Group One,

I knew I did not belong there. Also, someone from you guys told someone who then told me everything that happened on that Christmas night. Thanks for voting me out as if you are the house of congress or some shit. Childish. I hope you guys are doing okay.

Dear Friend Group Two,

I found a home in you guys when I first met you. I was blinded by the longing for belonging. It took me years to be able to stand up on my own. I heard the whispers of you wanting to kick me out of the friend group as soon as I left for Chicago. Cowards.

Dear M,

Thank you for kicking me out of the group chat and the friend group. I went to the movies right after that.

Dear I,

I'm not sorry. I deserved better.

Dear Old Me,

Let's move on. Please.

2003 KIDS AIN'T KIDS ANYMORE

All I wanted when I was a kid
was to be old and on my own.

But all things said it ain't so bad,
I find it cool that no one understands
Who am I or what do I want? Because neither do I.

I never celebrated my childhood enough,
so I'll cherish and enjoy it before all this stops,
because we are no longer kids, but we're not adults.

So I'll stay up late and kiss strangers I'll regret.
Where I used to play, I'll smoke cigarettes.
We watch the TV games and place our bets.

This is the best and worst age to make mistakes.

GOOD LUCK EX FRIENDS AND LOVERS

I had a lover when I was young
but called it quits one week before
February the fourteenth.

I know the timing could not have been worse.
It was all calm, and I caused the storm.

Some friends hated it when I was around:
they laughed while I bled on the ground,
so I cut all ties and moved away.

I loved this person, but they didn't reciprocate.
Now, why would I stay?

I wish good luck to my old friends and lovers,
because all I do now that what we had is over,
is mail letters with the wind,
because I don't know where you live.

SALTY

I met the love of my life in the spring
and perhaps even sprinkled some hints.
They made me feel glad I exist.
But I can't tell them! I've gotta resist!

It felt kinda wrong, felt a little shame,
but I was chasing after those eyes
and even though it was very clear,
I knew I was running towards my demise.

When they fell for somebody else
I hated them right there and then.
But now I'm the sea,
salty and faraway.

SWEET

The one I loved never pointed out the sweets
or thanked the chef for the pastry.
I'll die never having been acknowledged or seen
for giving you something so sweet and tasty.

NERVOUS MESS

My nerves get the best of me:
that's why I hide behind poetry,
or behind a movie screen.

My words shake into noises
that sound backwards.
My hands shake like earthquakes.
I try to think, but it's abstract.

I fail, I fall,
I try to get up
but I stumble
once more.

The world looks at me; the world sees a joke.
Should I try to speak at all?

LOOK, A BIRD!

Distract me while the world fucking burns,
when all that's good turns bad then worse,
come and hug me 'til it no longer hurts.

I want to be vulnerable
but I'm afraid you'll do
the unforgivable.

I understand that
to take, I have to give.
We can get serious later,
but for now, just distract me.

BEDROOM POEMS

I've written most of my books
sitting in bed.
I've illustrated most of them
on the toilet.

I loved every room I've ever slept in,
because it's creatively fun and quiet.

Sure, they all start blank and boring,
but that means endless stories.

I lay in bed headfirst,
head over stacked pillows,
computer overworked.
My writing process is simple.

The dry tears in my bed,
the punch marks on my walls,
make this the perfect place
to write every poem.

UNEMPLOYED WORKAHOLIC (I'M HAPPY)

Being happy means I'm unemployed.
Sadly, the world hates the happy.
I have nothing to write about if overjoyed.

I rely on my sadness and sorrow
to still have a career tomorrow.
I just got home, and I'm afraid
to either lose my job or lose you.

I'm happy and dancing,
singing while cooking,
pretending I'm in a movie
while I'm walking down Clark Street.

I'm afraid that this might go away,
but I'll handle it if it does...
and write about it.

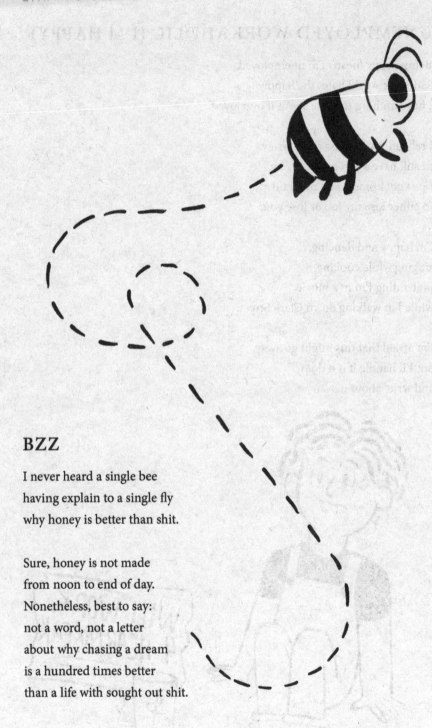

BZZ

I never heard a single bee
having explain to a single fly
why honey is better than shit.

Sure, honey is not made
from noon to end of day.
Nonetheless, best to say:
not a word, not a letter
about why chasing a dream
is a hundred times better
than a life with sought out shit.

ARTSY KID

When am I gonna stop
trying to climb to the top
just because I wanna make art?

I scream at the top
of my lungs, 'til they pop:
"This is something I made from the heart."

I'll celebrate little successes,
but there's no one in tuxes or dresses.

The question that haunts me aloud is:
"Would I still do this if there
was absolutely no one in the crowd?"

I'm enjoying the making.
You say the promoting's annoying,
but it's only preventing me from doing it again.

SMOKE SIGNALS

I say nobody looks for me,
but I hide when someone does.
It's not that there's nobody.
It's that it's not you doing the hunt.

CIGARETTE BREAK

Lately, Chicago's been my ashtray,
been outside roaming on my own.
I exchanged glances with an old man
as if it were me when old.

GLASS HOUSE

Our glasshouses are different.

Your bricks are made of
broken-beer-bottle glass.
Throw one stone
and the house goes boom!

My bricks are made of
polycarbonate that kicks ass!
Might shoot a million bullets,
but my glass is bullet-proof.

ADULT SHIT

I've got friends outside my age range.
Though I'll eventually get to their stage.
Right now, I'm just a cameo,
on a show where everybody acts their age.

It's like I have an older brother
and he invited me to come.
Excited for the idea of it
but while I'm here, I wish it'd be done.

I feel like a wandering child
in the market's alcohol aisle.
I stood with people talking
and did not even do it in style.

It's the cool paintings,
the guitars, the decor.
It's the cool-patterned rug
that's on the floor.

When you're old, but not old enough.
You like apple juice boxes, but also cigarettes.
I pretend to be tough, but only end up with regrets.

EXCUSE ME, SIR?

After my parents dropped me off
and I was in college all alone,
I circled to a nearby store
to buy groceries on my own.

I was walking down the aisle
when a boy and his sister inquired
if the headphones they picked
were the ones that came with a wire.

I helped the little boy and girl
resolve their little qualm.
And after they got what they needed,
they ran back to their Mom.

I got out of the store
and ran alone back to my dorm.
While my family
was at the O'Hare airport.

BOOM

What you say, your intentions were,
will never in a billion years compare
to a single action showing you care.
You see me mad and say "it's unfair" —
like I can read your fucking mind.
Another day beyond repair.

TALK TOO MUCH

I just spilled my guts to a stranger,
and trusted this person with all I carried.

I gave it to him.
He looked at it.
He listened to all I said.

He then took all I carried
and threw it in the ocean.
Just like that.

I've been carrying silent heartbreak,
internalized hate for me,
troubles since childhood,
things I never gave myself a break for.

All I've carried for ages, gone in a second.

I've cared too much,
I've loved myself too little,
He gave me the hug I never gave myself.

I know in a few months or some time,
he'll not remember or talk to me,
but it was nice to pass the time.

I shared all the cards I was dealt with
to a tall, strange, white, blonde guy.

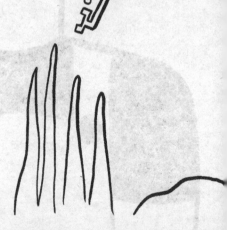

GLITCH

I wasn't supposed to stop by
I didn't know your name, but still.

My system needed loving,
your system was high as hell.
So, I elevated myself to your level.

We talked and almost kissed
if it wasn't for my fucking friend
who came and interrupted this.

I smiled the whole way home
hoping you'd remember me
in the midst of your marijuana fog.

I used my telephone and internet
to stalk you while it was killing me.
The photo of you, I zoomed in on it
and begged the universe for a chance.

MAKE ME A ROBOT

I was a cold and calculated machine,
but you found a way to warm the wires.
You came along and grew a heart in me,
promised me something that would never expire.

I might've been a machine
but holy shit, you were colder than me.
I'd take you to the sun and die
if it meant you showed a little appreciation.

DEATH DROVE BY

Today, death drove past me,
though it could've been closer,
death waved hello to me,
as it almost ran me over.

It passed me by
outside my house
when I was about to cross the street.

Had I not forgotten
where my keys were
I would now be below six feet.

Make no mistake
death drives in style
using every single cent
that all his chores
bring to his home
from the people's lament.

So, hello death,
I'm okay, but I am not quite done.
I'll see you
when you're ready to take me at dawn.

ROCKSTAR

When he started,
he started slow.
Hid his face and voice
for fear of mockery.

When he got comfortable
he showed his face,
and greeted friends and strangers.

When he had ideas
he executed them
alone in his bedroom.

He waved and talked to a camera
every single time he could.
Because that was better than silence.

He locked himself in his room
every weekend while the kids played.
He would watch, rewatch, and polish
videos he had done in his bedroom with his phone.

He was happy.
At least, that is what he told himself.

He had terrible moments.
When he crashed,
everyone cheered.

Everyone who to his face
congratulated him.
Picked apart every word he said,
and every action from him.

When he stood,
he stood on a mountain of the things he did.
Countless videos on the internet were his reputation.

People knew him,
yet did not know him at all.

He made films now
instead of videos.
He did books now
instead of napkin poems.

He took what he learned
and took him to places he'd never been.

The kid who once piled boxes
and angled his phone down on his desk
to chit-chat and vent and talk and converse
was no longer that child and lived faraway.

 ElCharlieLerma
81 subs

MARIA

"Keep your head up,
for you are not a loser."
"If you want something,
you have to be the best."

My Mom was the unsung hero of my life.

She taught me lessons
I asked her questions,
about where to go
and how to be.

I'm in college now and far
from my mother's hugs and kisses.
She's everything. Both a queen and *a princess*.

I miss just us going out to eat,
and the way we cursed bad drivers' skills.
I'm 20, but still, would hold your hand in the street.
I'm 20, and you still help me swallow big pills.

I sit alone in my college cafeteria
and miss your homemade cooking.
I need a hug, but I want it from you.

As a kid, your signature was insane
you signed 'Lalys' as your name
but your autograph was something
I could never in a thousand years recreate.

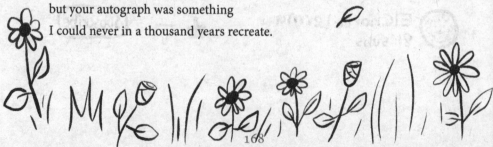

You are far but you're right here,
in every corner of my room.
You're in the sun that wakes me up,
and when I look up at night at the moon.

I sometimes wish I had stayed
to see you every day.
But I know you wanted me
to leave the nest someday.

And I wait for the flight to come,
so I will board and ride a plane home.

I want to tell you all the stories
and show you all the fun things I did.
I want to tell you how I've applied
every skill you taught me as a kid.

You liked to sign your name a million times
on paper while speaking on the phone.
Now I do the same now that I'm grown.
I do the things you do when I'm alone.

When I leave, half of my heart stays.
I live counting down all the days
until I come back home to see your face.

Dear Mom,
I don't know better yet.
For I'm still a kid.
Please teach me more of everything.

THE LONGEST TIME

Eternity followed — a second worth a thousand years of waiting.

LOGIC GIRL, GUTS BOY

I met this girl
but she's afraid to jump.
As it gets serious
the breaks are pumped.

I'm a simple day-to-day guy
but she's already scared for when we part.
But if we give it a try
we might prove her worst fears wrong.

I'm walking fast to meet you downstairs,
I see you smiling in the lobby chairs.
For you have an energy you can't dismiss
but in my room, we do everything but kiss.

Please take my hand and jump
if we don't fly and fall off the cliff
we'll be each other's lesson
but gone will be the 'what if.'

SUNNY

Sunshine, my sunshine.
Everyone's, but never mine.
Aren't you the thing
I can't avoid, but can never have?

Dear lovely sunshine,
tell me why I can't live without you.
For I'm not a sunflower,
but you might make it true.

Music takes to make-believe movie scenes
and you and I are the stars.
Tell me when you and I will have something
that we can call only ours?

Sunshine, my sunshine,
everybody needs and loves you.
I know I'm not that important.
So tell me, what can I do?

OUI'D

Sometimes I feel I give more than I get
but I know the world isn't in my debt.

People come, people go,
but who will stay?
Not my paper friends
that wash away with the rain.

I like the feeling of being missed
'cause lately, I've just been dismissed.
I talk, but everybody's a wall,
and I'm not someone they can't resist.

In my living room and in the clouds, all at once.
When I come down,
I feel my dry lips,
dangerously empty stomach, and broken heart.

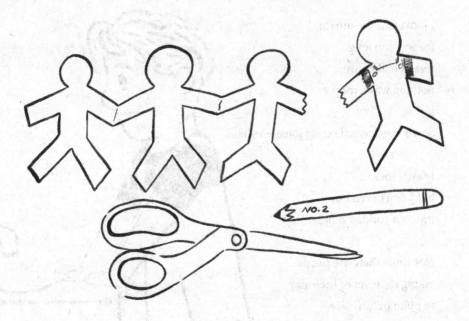

SHIRTLESS

It started before my underdog days,
thought it was a phase.
My little body started to change.

I grew scared of
swimming pool parties.
For I wasn't part of the
Kens and the Barbies.

So I stayed inside.

I bought bigger clothes to cover
every inch of my body
because I hated
my arms and tummy.

So I spent so much more cash.

I looked in the mirror
for way too long.
Just to make sure
nothing was wrong.

So my eyes started seeing something else.

I say "I love me",
but I don't even buy
my own goddamn lies.

Not while there are people
taking time out of their day
to point out my size.

DEAD GOLDFISH

There are people like the kids
who get goldfish at the county fair.
They play with it for a day,
then leave it for their Moms to care.

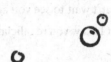

Don't act like a child,
follow up with your actions.
Because it feels like I'm drowning
after every single interaction.

I don't want your friends
to poke you when you've forgotten.
I don't want you to eat what I made
long gone after it's rotten.

You should've never picked me up,
should've picked another prize.
For all I am is a county fair goldfish,
and I met my demise.

WALK OF SHAME

I'm walking down Clark Street
from someone else's place.
I got the clothes from last night
and a smile you can't erase.

All this snow,
yet I can't even feel the cold.
For my heart's mind
has other things to mentally behold.

Daydreaming so much,
I had to wait another minute
to cross the street, I missed the sign.

I can't wait to see you again someday
but today, you're officially mine.

ALL Y TAKEN!

Where's the shame in that?

BEST THURSDAY

It was the best Thursday ever
with my hand wrapped around your thumb.
I was a fragile dandelion, and you hand me to Mom.

What's that wooden rectangle
that takes me to another place?
What's that exact silhouette of me
on the floor following me everywhere?

I don't know who you are,
but I'll find out soon.
It all started on a Thursday,
the 12th of June.

Two years passed after I arrived,
and one day, you two came home
with another baby in your hands.
Who's this guy who crashed the poem?

Another bed is added to my single room,
I have a brother now; how cool.

Our house has room for us to run;
and to play, jump, and get hurt.
My Dad dealt with the scary bugs.
I don't know what my Dad did, but it worked.

I peed on the bed,
or had nightmares, then,
woke you way past midnight.

I'd get in with you in bed.
And in between you two
I would sleep very tight.

Sure, I fucked up
like every child does.
The only reason
I learned it was because…
I have the best pair of mentors,
I get to call Mom and Dad.

I know you've traded everything
just to see me smile.
And I'll return the favor,
it will only take a while.

I have the best Mom and Dad
this world has ever seen.
To see a copy like them,
you'll need a time machine.

And maybe one day
I'll bring home a newborn babe.
I'd try to be just like my Dad,
but I would be a cheap copy of someone great.

Los amo.

WHEN I DIE

When I die, give what's left of me away.
Take my bones, my clothes, and cash
and make sure those who need it are okay.

If there is any need to cry,
please wipe those tears away.
There's no need to be sad by
me in a better place to stay.

I heard bees, gossip, and songs
and ate anything that looked divine.
I look back at everything
while I'm standing here in line.

So, when I die, give all my money away,
give it to the homeless on the streets
and make sure they have a better today.

I enjoyed this little game
that some people call life.
I got no beginner's luck,
but I turned out pretty fine.

I hope you're looking your best
as you say your last goodbye.
I can't wait until we get to meet
in the skies again, eye-to-eye.

Before I finally close my eyes,
will my words have any weight?
Will you remember everything
this mouth has ever written or said?

I refuse to have my thoughts
come with me to the grave.
So I will lay them here to rest
and have them forever on display.

Will I look back at these adultish years
when my blood has stopped to run?
Will I be grateful for the lessons learned
after being dragged through the mud?

So, when I die, this is the task I'll leave.
Take me to my Monterrey home
and let my ashes fly with the wind.

EVERYTHING MAKES SENSE

I got into the job as a teenager.
I might stay here 'til I die.
Playing with art supplies in my bedroom
was the only thing that got me by.

I started playing with cameras
and stopped going out on Fridays.
Because it's better to talk to a lens
than to people who didn't want me there.

Now, they got me thinking.
I got no chance to shine,
I'd never be able to survive.

But if I never try,
I'll never truly be alive.
But what if this turns out phenomenal?

Is this what dreams are made of?

I wrote away at the back of the classroom
to maybe try and stay calm,
but every teacher hated what I was doing
so they sent a note to my Mom.

Labeled as problematic
for just being in my world.

Alone at home with the internet,
it soon became my best friend.
I told countless stories
to strangers I wanted to impress.

It's an endless fire
of an endless desire
to live every hour
writing at my desk.

If you love what you do,
you'll never work a day in your life.
Everything you love
can be your new job; you decide.

And they tried to take it away
but it's everywhere I'm in,
it's in the notebooks and the napkins
it's in every atom of my skin.

It's in my walls and in my heart,
it's on every single late-night walk,
it's the best thing I can't escape.

I have to say, it's thanks to you
I get to live doing what I do.
Just know you saved me
and turned me into someone new.

Whoever's afraid of dying,
let them not be born.
Why not try getting everything,
before everything is gone?

CARLOS LERMA

WHAT'S MY MIDDLE NAME?

Run as far away
as your feet will allow you.
He's a hurricane,
and you're just made out of paper.

Break off all ties,
he could never be a weeping groom.
He's a Chicago roaring breeze,
and you're the brightest candle in the room.

Alone in his tower, locked away.
Do you really want to join him?
He's a monster not meant to be loved.
He lives in a solitude that's grim.

People don't even know my middle name,
yet that's enough to uphold all their claims.

NOBODY KNOWS MY FEBRUARY SECRET

I'm a private guy, sure,
but I want to tell everyone.
So I tell everyone, but not quite—
My moving drawings and poems do the talk.

See what I'm saying?

You're shy and coy,
but are you looking at me today?
Other pretenders dance in bars and clubs;
but all you want from me is a simple walk.

You playfully kiss my forehead;
but is this a joke or a hidden clue?
Hints hide in plain sight for me to decode,
already in my mind under review.

I'm not good at keeping secrets—
I talk to my notebooks all too often,
but bury everything in a book; now it's coffin.

I was not good at keeping you—
The picture I had of a perfect summer softens.
I had a voice that told me it could happen, but it was bluffing.

LOS ANGELES

Quick, quick, tell me what's the place
where all dreams escape the mind into your hands?
Quick, quick, tell me where to go
to turn my rusty life shimmery and grand?

I've heard of it, never met it—
An urban legend among my peers.
You'll stumble upon it,
but not until you're of the highest tiers.

I stumble into the city of angels,
as a humble mortal trying to grow wings.
I saw it for three moons, but I want to stay for years.

I walk Sunset Boulevard dressed for Chicago weather.
All I hear in my mind,
are my foes hoping I'd never found this land of treasure.
The place where their entrance would be denied.

Los Angeles came knocking at my door,
I'm glad I met you, but now I want more.

NEVER HAUNT YOU AGAIN

There was one I would've died for,
but they only saw me as just another old bore.
If I wanted to get close, I ought to be a ghost.
Invisible and quiet, without to disturb.

ACKNOWLEDGMENTS

To my parents, Carlos & Maria. My number one fans and the two people who showed me how the world is. The world is good, but the world is ruthless. Thank you for all the lessons, rides, and love.

To my brother Alejandro: I hope I was a good example growing up because now I have nothing left to teach you. I've learned more about you in the last few years on how to survive socially in this world. So, thank you!

To my best friend: I'd be dead without a loyal friend like you. Thank you for taking care of me when I needed it most, for the excellent advice, the good times, and the good food. Thank you for showing me new places, teaching me new things, and letting me realize the most extraordinary people are the ones who read.

To S, X, M, D, R: I'll try to live the rest of my days giving back all the love you've given me. I'm grateful you've always been with me over the years and the turmoils, over the challenges and heartaches.

To the ones that broke my spirit, ruined my day, and broke my heart: you can't take credit for my sadness; I earned this entirely on my own. I was the one that could've and should've left but didn't for believing water can be dry if you talk them out of it.

To L, my partner in crime in this new place, thank you for being with me since day one. You've taught me so much about life and how to live it fearlessly. We'll both be rockstars in the end.

To my college friends, you know who you are. After coming to another country, you guided me, befriended me, and pointed out when my English was bad. Thank you for letting me be your friend.

To S: I'm glad and grateful we met because had we never met, I'd have nobody to laugh with in Spanish.

To my fans and supporters: I'd be nowhere without the love and care you give me. The love you give to everything I do pushes me every time a little bit further. You are my fireflies; the love you give me inspires me every day.

ABOUT THE AUTHOR

Carlos Lerma is a Mexican award-winning writer-director and author known for his collection of live-action and animation original films. With a passion for storytelling since childhood, he started uploading videos to the internet from his hometown, Monterrey, Mexico, and naturally transitioned into narrative and poetic storytelling a few years before moving to the US. His films offer a unique writing style because all films stem from his personal life stories. Currently residing in Chicago, IL, Lerma continues to chase his dreams in entertainment and literature.

Printed in the USA
CPSIA information can be obtained
at www.ICGtesting.com
LVHW030529290524
781383LV00010B/630

9 798869 089113